To
Stephanie

From
Mom and dad

Date

Through-the-Day Stories

PRECIOUS MOMENTS™

Through-the-Day Stories

Stories by V. Gilbert Beers
Illustrations by Samuel J. Butcher

BAKER BOOK HOUSE
Grand Rapids, Michigan 49516

First printing, February 1991
Second printing, October 1991

Library of Congress Cataloging-in-Publication Data

Beers, V. Gilbert (Victor Gilbert), 1928–
Precious Moments : through-the-day stories / stories by V. Gilbert Beers ; illustrations by
Samuel J. Butcher.
    p.   cm.
Summary: Brief story-poems heighten our awareness of the special features of wake-up
time, mail time, chore time, family time, and other such times of the day, highlighting God's
role in all aspects of our lives.
  ISBN 0-8010-0992-8
  [1. Day—Fiction. 2. Christian life—Fiction. 3. Stories in rhyme.] I. Butcher, Samuel J.
(Samuel John), 1939– ill. II. Title.
  PZ8.3.B393Pr   1991
  [E]—dc20   90-1265
                                                     CIP
                                                     AC

Printed in the United States of America

Contents

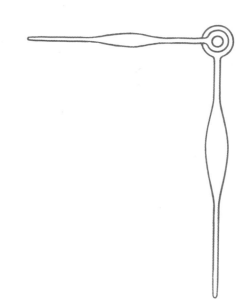

Letter to Parents

Morning was always a delight for me as a child. In the summer the crowing of a rooster announced the birth of a new day. House wrens joined their voices, along with robins and cardinals. One by one farmyard animals added their sounds, awakening a sleepy world. A symphony had begun, announcing a new day.

These morning songs were graced by the long rays of the sun, streaking across my bedroom window in our old farmhouse. Each ray lit something in my room in a unique way, highlighting that which was usually subdued.

Breakfast scents drifted up from my mother's homespun kitchen—bacon or sausages, eggs, pancakes, or waffles. My mother was not a gourmet cook. We had plain farm cooking. But those smells were ecstasy to a growing boy.

The songs of a new day had begun. The day was mine to enjoy . . . or ignore. I seldom ignored the wonders of each day because each signaled to me some remarkable gift from God.

Wisely, God chose to divide our lives into bite-size chunks called days. Think how oppressive life here on earth would be if it were one long chore for ninety or so years! God was wise also to divide the day into special parts with special interests: morning, noon, evening, night. Each held me captive as a child with its wonderfully unique presentations. Each was mine to enjoy. As you reflect on days gone by, or perhaps even on today, you may feel as I did.

Writing this book has helped me relive the joy of each day. It has reminded me again that the processes of a day are something of great delight if only we will participate in them. I recognize that it was the Creator who made the day, and night, and all variations between.

If this book will stir in your child, and you, a new joy for "the day that God has made," it will have served its purpose.

V. Gilbert Beers

1

*Who
Wakes Up
the Day?*

Who wakes me in the morning,
  So I can start to play?
  My mother does!
But who wakes up the day?

Who turns the light on in my room,
  So I can have some fun?
  My father does!
But who turns on the sun?

Who starts the water in my bath,
  And closes up the drain?
  My mother does!
But who turns on the rain?

Who fixes things when they don't work,
  When stuff gets cracked or curled?
  My father does!
But who repairs the world?

Who hangs my clothes for me to see,
  Right there before my eyes?
  My mother does!
But who hangs up the skies?

Who wakes the day,
Turns on the sun?

19

Makes sure the bath
For the world is begun?

Who fixes a world
When it needs repair?
Who hangs the skies,
Away up there?
God does!

Have you thanked your loving mother,
   for getting you up to play?
Have you thanked your loving father,
   for working things out okay?
And have you thanked your heavenly
      Father,
   for waking up the day?

2

*When
I
Wake Up*

When I wake up
in the morning,
Does sleepytime
go to bed?

And when
   I go to sleep
   tonight,
Must it get up
   instead?

3

*A Day
Is Like
Growing Up*

At sunrise the day is a baby

At breakfast, it's a kid like me;

By noon it's like a mom or dad,

And grandparents' time is at three.

At sunset the day is fading
At bedtime we say good-bye;

When stars shine bright,
it's like the time
When we live with God
on high.

4

*Don't Look
at the Way
Things Look*

"Don't look
at the way
things look,"
that's what
my mother
will say.

"Don't look
at what they are
this morning,
just watch
how
they
change today."

A caterpillar is just a caterpillar.
  It can't be a beauty queen.
But things do change and rearrange;
  what you'll see
  is not what you've seen.

A butterfly makes us ooh and sigh,
  as it flies into the sky.
You'd never know how it could grow
  from that wormy little guy.

"Don't look at the way you look,"
that's what my dad will say.
"Don't look in the mirror
and see what you see,
just look at the picture
and see what you'll be."

A barbell is just a barbell.
  You can buy one down at the store.
But if your chest isn't overly blessed,
  you can work up a whole lot more.

"Don't look at the way you look,"
  this birdie
    said to its egg.
"Don't look at your shell
and think you're not well;
  you'll soon fly to Winnipeg."

An egg is just an egg.
  It's not egg-citing today.
But when the shell breaks,
a new life awakes,
  and a beautiful bird soars away.

"Don't look at the way you look,"
  that's what I want to say.
"Don't look in the mirror
and see what you see,
just think of all that you can be."

A kid is just a kid.
　That's what you may want to say.
But the Creator's not done
with what he's begun.
　He will finish a little each day.

38

5

Read Me a Rhyme About Time

If the clock on my wall has hands,
Where are its fingers and toes?

If the clock in the kitchen has a face,
Does it ever blow its nose?

If the clock downstairs has a twelve,
Why doesn't it have thirteen?

When my teacher says, "Stop killing time,"
Does she know I'm not that mean?

When your father says, "time flies,"
Have you ever seen its wings?

If the bird on your clock can say "cuckoo,"
Do you think it also sings?

If the clock in the den has a second hand,
Where does it keep the first?

And if your clock rings with alarm,
Does it fear the very worst?

My mother says our grandfather clock
Strikes every single hour.

I hope he doesn't strike too hard
To show he has clock power.

If your clock starts to run too fast,
Would you even try to catch it?

And if it cut its little hand,
How would you ever patch it?

If your clock could talk when it tells time,
What else do you think it would say?

Do you think it would like to talk with you,
And tell you it's time to pray?

6

*A
TICK-TOCK
Time
Rhyme*

Why does my clock say
    TICK
    TOCK?
The watch on my wrist says
    TICK
    TICK.
Shouldn't my clock say
    TOCK
    TOCK?
Or would it prefer
    CLOCK
    TOCK?

Then should my watch say
    CLICK
    TICK?
Or play a trick and say
    CLICK
    CLICK?

I wonder what makes my
    CLOCK
    TICK.
When time flies fast, does it
    TICK
    QUICK?
Well, this is enough of
    TICKS and
    TOCKS
From tick-tock things like
    WATCHES and
    CLOCKS.
I'm going to stop this
    TICK-TOCK
    RHYME.
Because
  I
    have
      just
        run
          out
            OF
              TIME.

7

Upside-Down Breakfast

The girl next door
    sits on the floor
While the family
    dines at the table.
She insists they
    call her Marabelle
When her name
    is really Mabel.

45

With her plate on her legs she eats her eggs
By sipping them through a straw.
You'd think they'd be boiled or easy-over
But actually they're almost raw.

She bakes a cake with one cornflake
And gobbles it all for brunch.
You'll never guess what kind of mess
She puts together for lunch.

Oh, one thing more, this girl next door
Eats thirteen eggs for dinner.
With a diet like that she should get fat
But she claims she is getting thinner.

She gobbles her food and thinks it is good
And wants my breakfast, too.
But it's all okay, because they say
She's moving next door to you!

8

A Breakfast Fit for a King or Queen

"Time for breakfast," Mother called.

Annie and Arnie ran down the stairs. Before Mother could say "hurry," they were sitting at their places at the table.

"What are we having this morning?" Annie asked.

"Surprise," said Mother. "But it's a breakfast fit for a king or queen."

"That's sounds great!" said Arnie. "But what would a king or queen like for breakfast?"

Father smiled when he heard that. "Do you think a king or queen would like waffles?" he asked.

Arnie patted his tummy. "This king would!" he answered.

"So would this queen," said Annie. "Anyone would like waffles!" You've probably guessed that Annie and Arnie both like waffles for breakfast.

"Not anyone," said Father. "Do you remember the horse you rode last summer? He would rather have a bucket of oats for breakfast. I don't think he would like waffles."

"Poor horse," said Annie. "I'd hate to eat a bucket of oats."

"That's because you're Annie," said Mother. "If you were a horse you would love a bucket of oats for breakfast. That's the way God made a horse. And he made Annies and Arnies to like waffles. Different kinds of animals, or people, like different kinds of food."

"Kitty and Puppy sometimes like the same things we do," said Annie.

"Some things," said Mother. "But I think Puppy would rather have dog biscuits than the cherry pie I made for dessert tonight."

"Yuk! I'd hate to eat dog biscuits," said Arnie. "But I LOVE cherry pie."

"I love cherry pie, too," said Annie. "But I would hate to eat that cat food in a can that we give Kitty."

"Let's have a little breakfast guessing

game," said Father. "I'll give an animal and a food. Guess if that animal would like it."

"This sounds like fun," said Annie.

"Would a bunny eat carrots?" Father asked.

"Yes!" Annie and Arnie both shouted.

"But would Kitty eat carrots?" Father asked.

"No!" they both said.

"She might eat cooked carrots," said Father. "But I don't think she would eat raw carrots as a bunny would. Now, would a goldfish like an apple?"

"No," said Annie and Arnie.

"But would Kitty like to eat a goldfish?" asked Father.

Annie and Arnie remembered the time Kitty had tried to catch their goldfish. They were sure Kitty would eat it if she could.

"Would a cow like a hamburger or milk-shake?" asked Father.

Annie and Arnie both laughed. That one seemed almost silly.

"Would Annie and Arnie like cotton candy?" Father asked.

"Yes," they both said.

"Do you think a giraffe would like cotton candy?" Father asked.

They were both sure that a giraffe or ele-

phant or rhino or hippo would not like cotton candy.

"But why?" Annie asked.

"God made us to like certain foods so we will eat them," said Father. "He knows what is best for us."

"That's right," said Mother. "A bale of hay would give you a tummy ache. But hamburgers, fries, and shakes might not be very good for a cow, either. God knows what is best for each of us."

"I like candy bars," said Annie. "Does that mean they are best for me?"

"No," said Mother. "Horses like sugar, too. But no one would think of feeding a wonderful horse lots and lots of sugar. Some foods taste good, but we should be careful not to eat too much. God also wants us to learn to say no to things that taste good but aren't good for us."

"I'm glad waffles taste good and are good for us," said Annie.

"Thank you, God, for all good food that tastes good," said Arnie.

Annie and Arnie were very thankful for waffles that morning. They were sure they would not have been as thankful for a bale of hay!

Would you like a bale of hay for breakfast? Be sure to thank God for good food that tastes good.

9

My Magic Box Down at My Street

There's a magic box down at my street,
You should come and see it,
  it's really neat;
I stuff in a letter, away it goes,
Hopping or skipping on tippy toes.
It finds its way near or far,
To Chattanooga or Zanzibar.
How does it know where it should go
In New York City or Tokyo?
How does it know where to find you,
Does it run down each street
  and avenue?
Does it wear a wonderful thinking cap,
Or strap on a magical radar map?

There's more to this magical box
  that's really neat.
It grabs your letter on Anywhere Street;
And runs through the night,
  looking for me.
I'm sure that's a sight you'd love to see.
By morning mail time its little feet
Have found that box down at my street.
If you'll send a letter, I'll send one, too;
Perhaps we can each say,
  "I love you."

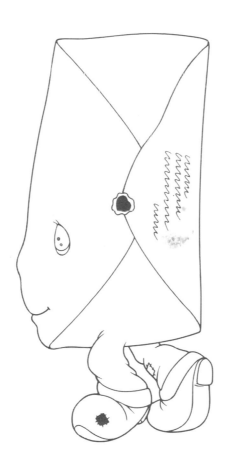

10

Which Face Are You Wearing Today?

"Ready for school, Mom," Kurt said.

"Good," said Mother. "But which face are you wearing?"

Kurt looked surprised. "I guess I'm wearing the only face I have," he answered.

"Well, there was another boy named Kurt running around the house before," said Mother. "I really couldn't tell who he was. He kept putting on different faces."

"What faces were they?" Kurt asked.

"When this other Kurt got up this morning, he put on his sunshine face," said Mother. "It had a big smile on it. That face

was warm and friendly, like the sun shin-
ing."

"I . . . I guess I was glad to get up and
get going," said Kurt.

Mother pretended that she didn't hear
that the other Kurt was really her Kurt.
"Then this Kurt boy couldn't find his
shoes," Mother said. "Suddenly he put on
a pickle face. You should have seen it! It

was long and sour and green, just like a pickle." Mother giggled.

Kurt frowned. He didn't like to think that he had a long, sour green face.

"Oh, yes," Mother went on. "That other Kurt put on a frown face, something like the one you're wearing now. That's because he had to go to school. You should have seen him."

"What other faces did this other Kurt wear?" asked Kurt.

"Let's see," said Mother. "There was a raindrop face. That's when he cried because he had to clean up his room a little. Oh, yes. There was also a pumpkin face. It was like a happy-go-lucky jack-o-lantern face. It really was nice."

"Mom, you do know that I was that other Kurt, don't you?" Kurt asked.

"Oh, my," said Mother. "I'm glad you told me. But you haven't told me which face you will wear to school."

Kurt laughed. "I'll wear my own face," he said. "But I hope it's like the sunshine face."

"It is already!" said Mother. She smiled as she watched Kurt and his sunshiny face run toward school.

By the way . . . which face are you wearing today?

11

Taking Pictures

Do you have a camera? Do you take pictures? Picture taking is fun. But did you know there are many ways to take pictures?

Casey has a camera. It's just an ordinary camera. It uses ordinary film. It takes ordinary pictures. Casey puts his ordinary pictures in an ordinary photo album. The photos help him remember what he did at school. They help him remember what his family did on special days. They help him remember what his family did on trips. Do you have lots of photos in a photo album?

What kind of pictures are they? What do you remember when you see them?

Casey also has two eyes. He looks at special things. If something is really special, Casey takes a "remember picture" and puts it in his mind. If he wants to remember that special something, he doesn't even look through a photo album. He doesn't turn a page and look for a photo. He just remembers it. He actually sees that "remember picture" as much as he sees a real photo. Do you have lots of "remember pictures" tucked away in your mind? Do you remember them often?

Casey has friends. He has a family. His friends and family watch Casey. When Casey does something special, Mother takes a little "remember picture" of Casey doing that special thing. If Casey does something naughty, a friend at school takes a little "remember picture" of Casey doing that naughty thing. Father takes "remember pictures" of Casey. So do his brother and sister. Many people have hundreds of "remember pictures" of Casey tucked in their minds. They can look at them any time by just remembering them.

God watches Casey every day. He sees everything Casey does. He knows everything Casey thinks. When Casey does good things, God sees every one of them.

God has not only "remember pictures," he even has something like a video tape of Casey's whole life. God's video tape even has pictures of all of Casey's thoughts. Casey squirms when he thinks about that. He would rather forget some of his words. He would rather forget about some things he has done. He would rather not remember some of his thoughts. Do you feel that way, too?

The next time you start to say a bad word, stop! Would you like a photo of you saying that bad word in God's photo album? The next time you start to do something bad, stop! Would you like a photo of you doing that in God's photo album? The next time you think a bad thought, stop! Would you like to see that photo of your thought in God's photo album?

There are many kinds of pictures. You and I should never say, think, or do anything if we wouldn't want to see a picture of it later.

Let's remember that the next time we're tempted to say, think, or do something not-so-good! Let's remember it, too, when we want to do something special.

12

There's a Mouse in My Lunch!

Did you have a mouse for lunch today? You probably didn't. But Alli did. Mother didn't put it in her lunch box. Alli didn't put it in her lunch box. You might guess that her teacher didn't put it there either.

But someone put a mouse in Alli's lunch box. And the mouse ate big holes in Alli's lunch. Alli wouldn't eat the rest of it.

Who put the mouse in Alli's lunch box? That's what Alli wanted to know.

"I'll get even with him," Alli said. She was sure it was one of the boys who teased her almost every day.

"Do you know who put the mouse in my

lunch box?" Alli asked each of her friends. "I want to get even with him."

She asked Sarah. She asked Amy. She asked Katy. But not one of her friends knew!

"Do you know who put the mouse in my lunch box?" Alli asked some of the boys. "I want to get even with him."

She asked Jason. She asked Jonathan. She asked Kevin. But not one of the boys knew!

Alli sat down at her desk. She began to cry. She was hungry.

Suddenly Alli felt a tap, tap, tap on her

arm. She looked up. Through her very wet tears she saw Sarah and Amy and Katy.

"Let's have lunch," said Katy. "We each want to share some of our lunch with you."

Alli was sure this was the very best lunch she had ever had. And she was sure these were the very best friends she ever had.

"Did you find out who put the mouse in your lunch box?" Sarah asked.

"No," said Alli. "No one will tell me."

"That's because you're asking the wrong question," said Amy. Then she whispered something in Alli's ear. Alli smiled.

Alli was almost through eating her lunch when she saw three boys. They were on the other side of the lunch room. They were watching her. One of them was laughing.

"That's Percival. I think he did it!" Alli whispered. "I'm going to ask him."

"Remember to ask the right question," said Amy.

Alli walked over to the three boys. They looked surprised. They didn't think she would do that.

"Do you know who put the mouse in my lunch box?" she asked sweetly. "I want to PRAY for him."

Percival gulped. The other two boys laughed. They looked at Percival. But Percival wasn't laughing. He looked down at the floor. His friends waited to see what he would do. Suddenly Percival ran out of the lunch room.

Alli put her lunch box on the shelf. She went back to her classroom. She kept thinking of the way Percival looked. She almost felt sorry for him.

After school Alli picked up her lunch box. Then she remembered that she had not thrown the scraps in the garbage.

Alli opened her lunch box. The first thing she saw was a piece of paper with some writing on it.

Alli opened the piece of paper. The writing said:

> I'm really sorry.
> Please forgive me
> and please pray for me
> and my family.
> My mother is sick
> and my father just lost his job.
> Percival.

What do you think Alli did at that very moment? What would you have done?

13

The Best Restaurant

"We're going out to eat lunch," said Mother. "But where should we go?"

"I want a nice restaurant," said Father. "It must have a beautiful setting with soft music. I want a place that is peaceful."

"And I want a place with great food," said Mother. "It should be the best food in any restaurant anywhere."

"I want a place where we can eat all we want," said Dean. "Some places send you away hungry."

"I want a place with great desserts," said Diane. "Some places just don't have great desserts."

The family began to think of the different restaurants that would have a great setting with soft music, the best food, all you can eat, and great desserts.

The Ritz had a great setting with soft music. But you couldn't eat all you want. Father said he couldn't pay for all Dean wanted to eat.

At The Down and Outers, you could eat all you want, but it didn't have a good setting with soft music.

Another place had good desserts, but not a nice setting. Still another place had great food, but very little for dessert.

Before long Diane and Dean began to argue. Mother and Father wanted to argue, but thought they shouldn't.

"But where can we go with a great setting and soft music, the best food, all you can eat, and great desserts?" asked Mother. "I can't think of a single place."

"Neither can I," said Father.

Mother, Father, Dean, and Diane all sat down and looked sad. Suddenly Dean had an idea. "I know where we can go!" he shouted.

Dean whispered in Diane's ear. Diane smiled. "That's it!" she said. "It has all of these things."

"Well, tell us!" said Mother.

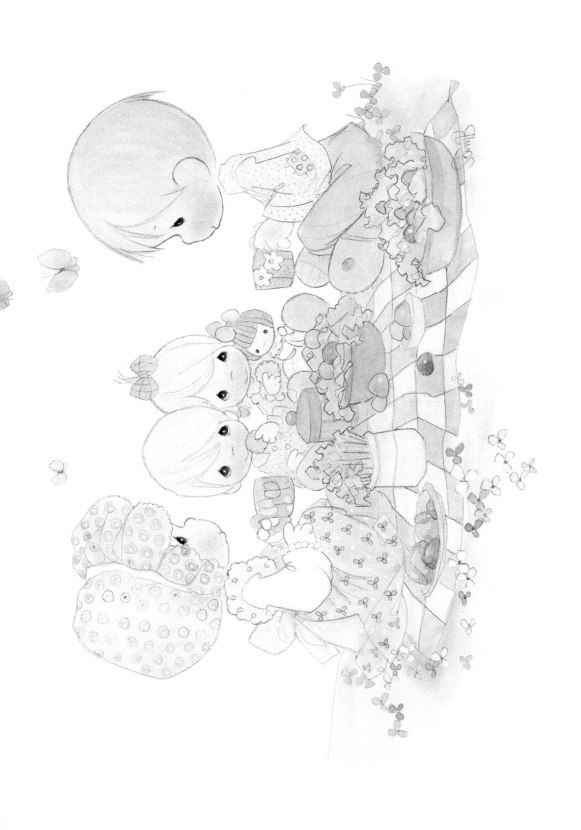

Diane whispered in Mother's ear. "You're right," she said. "That's the only place."

"Looks like I'm the last to know," Father said. "Okay, where is this magic restaurant?"

When Mother whispered in Father's ear, he smiled, too. "Of course!" he said. "It's the only place where you have a great setting and soft music, the best food, all you can eat, and good desserts."

So Mother and Father and Diane and Dean packed the finest picnic lunch you can imagine. They put in lots of great cookies for dessert. And they went to their favorite picnic spot in the woods.

The birds sang. The wind sighed in the trees. The squirrels chattered.

"Best music anywhere," said Father. "And look at this wonderful setting."

"Best food you can buy," said Mother, "even if I did fix it."

"I can eat all I want," said Dean.

"And look at these desserts," said Diane as she munched on a cookie. "But what's the name of this restaurant?"

"I think we should call it Our Family Restaurant," said Dean. So they did!

Can you think of a better name?

14

*Winning
and
Losing*

Would you win a game,
If you lost your best player?

Would you win an argument,
If you lost your best friend?

Would you win a race,
If you lost your sense
      of fairness?

Would you win someone's obedience,
If you lost their love?

Would you win the world's approval,
If you lost your family?

Would you win a promotion,
If you lost your job?

Would you win a battle,
If you lost the war?

Would you win a million dollars,
If you lost your good name?

Would you win the whole world,
If you lost your friendship with Jesus?

Winning something small
May be losing something great.

Winning something great
May be losing something even greater.

Read Matthew 16:26.

15

I Don't Want to Practice!

"It's not fair! I don't want to practice!" Lucy grumbled. "I just want to play the piano."

Lucy plunked a few notes on the piano. Then she began to daydream.

Lucy pretended that she was in a great hall. There was a beautiful grand piano in the center of the stage. And there were thousands of people in the audience.

These people were dressed up in their best clothes. Lucy smiled as she looked at them. The women wore the most beautiful evening gowns she had ever seen. The men were in tuxedos.

Then Lucy saw the sign. It had her name on it. This was HER great concert.

Lucy stepped out on the stage. The lights in the audience dimmed. Lights shined on her. Lucy bowed. Thousands of people began to cheer and clap. She bowed again. The people jumped to their feet. They clapped and shouted.

"Now this is the way it should be!" Lucy thought. "Who wants to practice when you can have this?"

Lucy walked across the stage. She sat on the piano bench. She was ready.

Suddenly a terrible feeling came over Lucy. What should she play? What could she play? The only thing she knew was the plunk, plunk, plunk piece her teacher had given to her. But she hadn't practiced it yet. She didn't even know plunk, plunk.

Lucy put her hands on the piano. "Plunk, plink, plunk," she played. It sounded terrible. People began to laugh.

Lucy tried again. "Plink, plink, plunk," it went this time. People laughed louder.

Once more Lucy put her hands on the piano keys. Her hands were shaking. Tears came into her eyes. All she could do this time was one little "plunk."

"Booo!" shouted the people. They laughed and laughed. Lucy burst into tears. She ran from the room and locked herself in the bathroom. She cried until she thought her heart would break.

"Is something the matter, dear?" a voice said softly. It was Mother's voice. Then Lucy saw that she was in her own bathroom in her own home.

"I . . . I need to practice," Lucy whispered to Mother.

Mother smiled. "I'm glad to hear you say that," she said. "What happened?"

Then Lucy told Mother about the pretend concert. "It was so beautiful at first," she said. "Then it was awful."

"If it helped you want to practice, it was a great concert," said Mother.

Lucy smiled. Then she bowed and went to her very own piano to practice. There was no one to listen to plunk, plunk, plunk, except her kitty.

16

Are You
Bigger
Than a
Bee?

If you think that big is better
Than tiny, small, or wee,
Have you ever made a honeycomb
Or ever stung a bee?

When you think you're more terrific
Than a lowly little fly,
Just try to make a mighty leap
A mile into the sky.

If you think that you are tougher
Than an itchy little flea,
Have you ever tried to tickle it,
And make it scratch its knee?

You may not like to hear it,
And perhaps you'll disagree,
But some things are done better by
A fly or flea or bee.

17

*Tigeroo
and
Monkey Two*

Said Little Mouse,
   "Come to my house,
We'll nibble on
   some cheese."
"I'd rather nibble
   on a mouse,"
Said Kitty,
   "if
      you
         please."

81

"Come play with me," said Busy Bee,
"We'll fly where it is sunny."
"I'll play with you," said Hungry Bear,
"If I can eat your honey."

"Come play with me," said Tigeroo,
"We'll dance with drum and pipes."
"We'll play with you," said Monkey Two,
"If we can change your stripes."

"Come play with me," said Lonely Jack,
"We'll play with balls and blocks."
"I'll play with you," said Playful Pup,
"But you must leave your box."

"Come play with me," said Woolly Lamb,
"I know you'll be content."
"I'll play with you," said Smelly Skunk,
"But you must wear my scent."

Some friends will play if you will say
And do strange things they do.
But please don't let their different way
Make you a different you.

18

What Is Play Time?

Do you ever have play time? I do. I'm having my play time now. Mom said so. She told me, "Run outside and play." So, I'm playing. But sometimes I'm not sure that I'm doing what I should do for play time. I'm not even sure what play time is. Do you know?

Do you think play time should be FUN TIME? I guess I have fun most of the time during play time. But sometimes I don't. I think I would have more fun if I had a friend to play with me during play time.

Is that what play time really is? Should play time really be FRIEND TIME? I would

like to play with my friends during play time. But my friends don't live near me. They live too far away to come over for play time. If they played with me, we could do things together. I think that would make play time more fun.

Maybe that's what play time should be! Play time is not just fun time. It's not even just friend time. I guess if I want to have fun with a friend, I must do fun things together with my friend. I guess play time is really TOGETHER TIME. If you could play with me during play time, we could do many things together.

We could make things together.
We could eat together.
We could sing together.
We could ride things together.
We could play games together.
And we could pretend to do fun things.

Do you suppose pretending is what makes play time so much fun together? Do you think play time should really be PRETEND TIME? When we pretend, we can think we're doing many things that we really can't do.

We can pretend we're brave knights fighting in great battles.

We can pretend we're sailing to wonderful places far away.

We can
pretend
that we're
grown-ups
like Mom
and Dad.

I asked Mom and Dad what we should pretend if we pretend to be them. Do you know what they said? They said we should pretend that we had a boy like me who

has FUN TIME
during play time,
has FRIEND TIME
during play time,
and TOGETHER TIME
during play time,
and even PRETEND TIME
during play time.

I guess that's what I'll pretend during play time today. I wish you could be with me, my friend, so we could pretend this together and have fun. If you can't, I'll pretend that you're here and that we're having fun pretending to do these things. Is that okay?

19

Wanda and Wendy

Wanda had a beautiful new puppy. She was so happy. But Wanda had a problem.

"I need a bowl of milk for Puppy," said Wanda. "Where will I find it?"

Wanda looked in her closet. But she could not find a bowl of milk there. She looked in her toy chest. But she could not find a bowl of milk there. She even looked in the refrigerator. But someone had taken all the milk. There wasn't even one drop of milk.

"Poor Puppy," said Wanda. "I must find a bowl of milk for him."

Wendy had a bowl of milk. She was happy with her bowl of milk. But Wendy had a problem.

"I need a puppy to share my bowl of milk," said Wendy. "Where will I find it?"

Wendy looked in her closet. But she could not find a puppy there. She looked in her toy chest. But she could not find a puppy there. She even looked under her bed. But she could not find a puppy there. Do you know why? Wendy did not have a puppy.

Wanda went out to look for a bowl of milk for her puppy.

Wendy went out to look for a puppy for her bowl of milk.

Wanda and Wendy saw each other on the sidewalk.

"Hi, Wendy," said Wanda. "I have a problem. Perhaps you can help me with it."

"Hi, Wanda," said Wendy. "I have a problem, too. Perhaps you can help me with it."

"I have a puppy, but I need a bowl of milk," said Wanda.

Wendy sighed. "I have a bowl of milk, but I need a puppy to drink it," she said.

"Oh, dear," said Wanda. "You really do have a problem. I hope you find a puppy."

"Oh, dear," said Wendy. "You really do have a problem, too. I hope you find a bowl of milk."

Suddenly Wanda looked at Wendy. Wendy looked at Wanda.

"Are you thinking what I'm thinking?" asked Wanda.

"I think I'm thinking what you're thinking," said Wendy. "I am if you're thinking what I'm thinking."

Wendy held out her bowl of milk. Wanda held out her puppy. Now Wanda had a puppy and a bowl of milk. Wendy had a bowl of milk and a puppy.

Soon Puppy had a full tummy.

Wanda and Wendy had a wonderful play time.

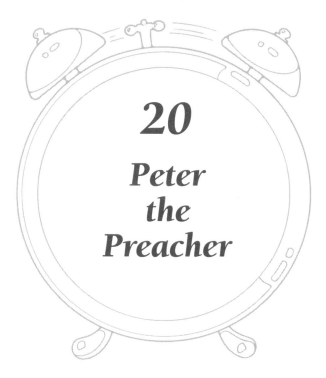

20

Peter
the
Preacher

"I'm going to be a preacher when I grow up," Peter told Mother.

"Really?" asked Mother. "That would be wonderful. But why do you want to be a preacher?"

"I want to dazzle the crowds," said Peter. "People will sit there and listen to every word I speak. They will sit with their mouths wide open. They will tell each other what a great preacher I am."

"Hmmmm," said Mother. "You may want to think of a better reason to be a preacher."

"Like what?" asked Peter.

"Like helping Jesus do his work," said Mother. "And like helping people find help for their problems in the Bible."

That didn't sound as exciting to Peter as dazzling the crowds. He could see all the people now. There would be thousands of them. They would all sit with their mouths wide open. They could repeat everything he said a week later.

Peter thought he would get started. He found an old orange crate and propped it up in the back yard. He invited some friends to hear him.

Peter's friends sat on the grass in front of him. Peter began to preach. He wasn't sure what he was saying or why he was saying it. But he kept talking anyway.

"Booo," said one of his friends. "Let's go play."

"Stop jabbering," said another. "You're not saying anything. I want a snack."

Peter's friends all walked away. Peter stood there behind his orange crate pulpit. He was alone. This didn't work the way he thought. They were supposed to sit there with their mouths open, listening to every-thing he said.

Peter found Puppy and Kitty. He plopped them in the grass in front of the orange crate. Peter began to preach.

Puppy sat still for fifteen seconds. But

when Peter shouted, Puppy put his tail between his legs and ran behind some bushes. Kitty ran the other way.

Peter looked at the empty spot on the grass. There weren't thousands of people. There wasn't even one dog or one cat. Nobody wanted to listen to him.

"I . . . I guess I'm a failure," said Peter. "Maybe Mother was right. Maybe I had the wrong reason to preach."

Peter bowed his head. He prayed a little. He asked Jesus to help him have the right reason to preach. But he cried more than he prayed. He felt terrible. He could see thousands of people walking away. Nobody wanted to listen to him. Nobody had mouths open, listening.

Suddenly Peter heard a soft "cheep, cheep" in front of him. He opened his eyes. There was a little bird sitting on his Bible. The little bird looked up at Peter. Peter stared at the little bird.

"I made everyone else come to hear me," said Peter. "But you came all by yourself. You came just when I needed a friend to listen to me."

Suddenly Peter knew that this little bird meant more to him than a hundred people who came but walked away. "Thank you, little bird," he said. "Thank you for coming to hear me."

"Cheep, cheep," said the little bird.
Peter preached softly to the little bird.
This time he didn't pretend that it was an
audience of thousands. He didn't pretend

that they sat there with their mouths open. He pretended that it was one poor person who wanted Jesus to help her. But Peter was so happy. The little bird sat there listening. It even had its mouth open!

"What do you think of my sermon?" Peter asked the little bird when he finished.

"Cheep, cheep," said the little bird.

Peter laughed. "I suppose it is cheap," he said. "I forgot to take the offering. But I feel better anyway. I preached to help Jesus instead of to dazzle the crowds."

That night Peter told Mother about the crowds that went away. He told her about the little bird that said, "Cheep, cheep."

Mother laughed with Peter when he told her that the little bird said his sermon was "cheap, cheap."

"But I learned something very important," Peter told Mother. "I learned that everything I do for Jesus must be to please him and help his people. I must never do his work to dazzle the crowds."

"That lesson didn't cost you a penny," said Mother. "Cheap, cheap!"

Peter and Mother had a good laugh together. Then they went to the kitchen for snack time.

21

Sailing to All the World

"What are you doing in that old tub?" Father asked.

"I'm sailing away to be a missionary," said Kevi.

"Now?" asked Father.

"Now," said Kevi. "We talked about missionaries in Sunday school this morning. So I'm ready to go right now!"

"Where are you going?" asked Father.

"To all the world," said Kevi.

"It's a big world," said Father. "Are you going to all the world at the same time? Or do you plan to start at one place?"

"I hadn't thought about that," said Kevi. "I

guess I'll start at one place first. How about Africa?"

"Africa sounds good," said Father. "But it's also a big place with many countries and many people. Where are you going in Africa? You need to decide on one place there."

"But how will I know which place to choose?" asked Kevi.

"There are many good ways," said Father.

"Listen to missionaries when they come here. Talk with them. Ask them questions."

"Today?" asked Kevi. "I'm ready to sail, you know."

"You may want to wait," said Father. "Missionaries won't be coming here today. You'll also want to read about the place where you are going. And of course you'll want to talk with the missionary organization that sends you."

"What's a missionary organization?" asked Kevi.

"Some men and women who work together," said Father. "They help missionaries go to the right places to work."

"How do they do that?" asked Kevi.

"First, they make sure you're ready to go," said Father. "They make sure you love Jesus. They make sure you want to tell people that he loves them."

"I love Jesus," said Kevi. "And I want to tell people that he loves them. Maybe I can go today."

"Then they will talk with you about your training," said Father. "Have you gone to Bible school or seminary? Have you had other special training to be a missionary?"

"I can't do all that today, can I?" asked Kevi.

"No, that takes several years after high

school," said Father. "You need to learn many things."

"Why can't I just read my Bible to the people and pray with them?" asked Kevi.

"You can," said Father. "But working as a missionary is much more than that. It's like being a pastor. Our pastor went to school several years after high school."

Kevi was quiet for a moment.

"A missionary organization also helps you get the money you will need," said Father.

"Why will I need money?" asked Kevi. "What will I do with it?"

"You will build buildings and keep them fixed. You will buy Bibles and teaching materials," said Father. "You also need to buy food and clothing for you and your family."

Kevi smiled. It was hard for him to think of having a wife and children.

Kevi jumped from his tub. "Looks like I'd better not sail today," he said. "I've got a lot of work to do first. While I'm working, I can tell my friends and neighbors about Jesus."

"First things first," said Father. "Now it sounds like the very first thing is dinner. I hear Mother calling."

"Let's go!" said Kevi. "All this travel has made me hungry."

22

*It's Best
to Do
the Best*

A turtle
and a reindeer
had a quarrel.
The reindeer
laughed
and called
the turtle
"slow."
"If I had that

101

funny horn
  that you got when you were born,"
   said the turtle,
    "You
     would
      see
       how
        fast
         that
         I
          could
          really
          go."

A lion and a pussy had a fuss.
  The lion laughed and called her "little
  kit."
  "If I had your grouchy roar,
   I could chase you out the door,"
    said the kitty.
     "You'd
      quit
       bragging
       and
        admit
        you
         need
         to
          split."

A girl and her mirror did not agree.
The mirror said, "You're still a little girl."
"With a gown and gorgeous car,
I could be a movie star,"
said the girl.
"You
would
show
a
lovely
lady
in
a
whirl."

What you are and what you wish are not
the same.
Do you reach too far for every star?
You may fuss and disagree.
But I hope that you will see
That
it's
best
to
do
the
best
with
what
you
are.

Telephone
Time

23

Holly's Hotline

"What did you do at school today, Holly?" her dad asked at dinner.

"We talked about hotlines in one of my classes," Holly answered. "I guess you have to be a very important person to have a special phone like that."

"Usually presidents and prime ministers have hotlines," said Dad. "That's so they can talk with each other about very important things."

"Do we have a hotline?" Holly asked.

Dad laughed. "Our line seems hot when you talk too long on the phone," he said.

"But it's not really a hotline. We don't need a hotline."

"Why?" asked Holly. "Don't we have important things to talk about?"

"Yes, we hope all that we say is important," said Dad. "But we don't talk with presidents and prime ministers, so we don't need a special phone."

Holly was quiet for a long time. Dad thought she was almost too quiet.

"But Dad," said Holly at last, "we talk with God about things. So why don't we have a hotline to him?"

Now Dad was quiet for a while. "I guess we do," he said. "It's called prayer. We don't need a phone to talk with God. He hears us without a phone."

"Even if we have something important to say to him?" Holly asked.

"Yes, even if we have something very important," said Dad.

That night when she was alone, Holly thought about school. She thought about the girl who made fun of her. She thought about hurting her finger at recess. She thought about not doing well when the teacher asked her to recite. She thought about spilling some juice on her good dress. Then a tear came into her eye.

Holly looked at the phone. "Maybe our phone really is a hotline to God," she said.

"Maybe no one really tried to call God on our phone."

Holly picked up the phone. She wasn't sure about God's phone number. Then she saw the letters with each number.

"I know what I'll do," said Holly. She touched 4. That had a G next to it. She touched 6. That had an O next to it. And then she touched 3. That had a D next to it.

"See, that spells GOD," said Holly.

Holly listened for God to answer. But it was quiet at the other end. Holly was sure that God was listening, so she began to tell him about her day.

"Do you think God listened on our hotline?" Holly asked Dad later. She told him what she had done.

"I'm sure he listened," said Dad. "He listens to all his important people. And you are one of his very important people."

"Just think!" said Holly. "A president or prime minister only has a hotline to another president or prime minister. But I have a hotline to God!"

"Makes you pretty special," said Dad.

24

***A Nap
Is Not
for Nat
(Me!)***

I have a hundred reasons why
A nap is not for Nat.
The afternoon was made for play.
Who wants to snooze away the day?
A nap is for a cat!

My mother wants me napping, but
A nap is not for Nat.
My toys get lonely when I'm gone.
They start to cry when I first yawn.
A nap is for a cat!

I wish my mother understood,
A nap is not for Nat.

I'll need at least a dozen drinks.
"That's thirteen times too much!" she
    thinks.
A nap is for a cat!

I think my mother is unfair,
A nap is not for Nat.
A thousand friends will come to play,
While I must sleep the day away.
A nap is for a cat!

I guess I must stop thinking that
        A nap is not for Nat.
        Because I heard what Mother said,
        "Stop arguing and get to bed!!!"
                So . . . I'll catnap
                    with my cat!

25

My
Pet
Parade

My mom will let me get a pet,
But I'm not sure which pet to get.

A hairy ape
   will help me
      scare
Those scary kids
   who shout,
      "I dare!"

111

But when I need a pocket, too,
I'll wish I had a kangaroo.

A cow will mow my grass for me,

Giraffes will
help me
climb a tree.

A frog will feast
   on flies and fleas,

A mouse will
   air-condition cheese.

A lion will guard my door at night,
A bird will help me fly my kite.

I'd like a rhino
on my team,

A unicorn will
share ice
cream.

But wait!

There's something I've not thought of yet!
If I'm not there, who'll feed my pet?

26
A New Friend

There was no one as sad
   as Grandpa McPhatt,
When he lost his pet pussy,
   a fat tabby cat.

But down at the pet shop
   a fellow named Ace
Said he'd find a pet kitty
   to take tabby's place.

There were
   Angora,
      Abyssinian,
         Malay,
            and Maltese,

Almost any conceivable cat
   that you'd please.
But Grandpa kept thinking
   about his one special cat,
No pedigreed Persian
   could ever top that.

So he left the pet store
   at the heart of the mall,
And he came back home
   with no cat at all.
He was feeling alone,
   with no one to share
His home and his food
   and his soft easy chair.

Then suddenly from somewhere a small
   face appeared,
A soft little fellow, long-tailed and pink-
   eared.
Then Grandpa decided there's a place in
   his house

For his new little friend
   who's a wee little
   mouse.

Now Grandpa
   McPhatt
   learned what you
   know, too,
That it's tough to lose
   someone
   precious to you.
And when someone's
   no longer
   there in your house,
You'll be glad for a
   friend,
      perhaps
         even
            a
            mouse.

27

Those Lovable, Unpredictable, Pettable Pets

Poor prickly pets aren't pettable

120

And scented skunks aren't sociable

Some pets aren't understandable

And some are unpredictable

Some pets are uncontrollable

But some are just plain lovable!

28

Cats
and
Dogs

Mother says my brother and I fight like cats and dogs. But I guess I didn't know how cats and dogs fight. So I decided to watch Kitty and Puppy.

The other night I stayed up late to watch how Kitty and Puppy fight when I go to bed. I thought they would put on little boxing gloves. I wanted to see if they fight that way. But they didn't fight at all. Puppy opened an eye once and looked at Kitty when she yawned. I think he wanted to be sure she was okay. Kitty yawned once. She opened one eye and looked at Puppy. I guess she wanted to be sure he was okay, too. Maybe I should watch my brother more to be sure he's okay.

This morning I accidentally stepped on Puppy's tail. He yelped a little yelp and crawled into the corner. Kitty went over and rubbed against him. I think she was purring. Do you think she wanted to make him feel better? Maybe I should help my brother feel better each time he gets hurt.

When I came home from school, my brother and I played ball. Kitty and Puppy played ball with us, too. My brother and I argued a couple of times. We even said some things brothers and sisters shouldn't say to each other. But Kitty and Puppy didn't argue. They didn't say one mean word to each other. Maybe my brother and I should watch how Kitty and Puppy play. Maybe we could learn some good things from them.

This afternoon I talked with Mother. I told

her what I had learned from Kitty and Puppy. Mother smiled and said she could be wrong. Maybe my brother and I don't fight like cats and dogs. Maybe we fight like brothers and sisters. And maybe, just maybe, we could learn some more good things from Kitty and Puppy.

29

Tubby and the Princess

Tubby was an ordinary pig. You would think an ordinary pig would think she is just an ordinary pig. But not Tubby. She thought she was a special pig. She thought she was even *more special* than ordinary special.

Perhaps that was because of the little patch Tubby wore. Or perhaps it was because she had a little collar with her name on it. Or perhaps it was because Tubby thought she was a little bit better than other barnyard animals.

As you might guess, Tubby had no

friends. Who wants a friend who thinks she is *more special* than ordinary special?

One day Tubby went out to find a friend. She wanted a special friend, not just an ordinary friend.

"Since I'm not just ordinary special, I want a friend who is not just ordinary special, too," said Tubby. "The friend I want must be a princess."

Most ordinary pigs would not say that. They would be glad to have ordinary friends. But not Tubby.

Tubby started across the barnyard, looking for the princess friend. Before long she met another pig. The other pig was sitting in a mud puddle.

"Are you a princess?" Tubby asked. "I'm looking for a friend. But she must be a princess."

The other pig laughed. She rolled over in the mud. Soon she was covered with it. "I guess I must be a princess," she said. "And this mud puddle is my palace." That seemed so funny to the other pig that she rolled over again and again in her "mud puddle palace."

Tubby did not think this was so funny. Actually, Tubby thought it might be fun to roll over in the mud. But she was sure the mud puddle was not a palace. And she was also sure this other pig was not a princess.

Tubby left the pig and walked over to the barnyard fence where a rooster was crowing as loud as he could. When the rooster saw Tubby, he stopped crowing.

"Well, what do you want?" he demanded. "You're interrupting my work, you know."

"I'm looking for a princess," said Tubby. Are you a princess?"

The rooster was angry when he heard this. He flew off the fence and glared at Tubby.

"Do I look like a scruffy little chick or an old hen?" the proud rooster shouted. He pecked at Tubby until she squealed and ran away.

Tubby was glad to get away from the rooster. She did not want a proud, angry friend like him.

Tubby went everywhere in the barnyard, looking for a princess friend.

She met an ordinary cow.

She met an ordinary horse.

She met an ordinary goat.

She even met an ordinary donkey.

But she did not meet one princess.

Tubby sat by a stump, feeling quite lonely. "I guess there isn't a princess in this barnyard," said Tubby. She didn't notice when a little skunk quietly climbed up on the stump.

"Hi!" said the little skunk.

When Tubby saw the skunk, she started to run. "Don't run," said the skunk. "I'm looking for a friend."

Tubby came back to the stump. She could see that the skunk did not want to hurt her.

"Are you a princess?" the skunk asked Tubby. "My new friend must be a princess."

Tubby wanted to say, "Yes, I am a princess." She wanted to tell the skunk that she was not just an ordinary pig. She wanted to say that she was even *more special* than just ordinary special.

But as the skunk looked into Tubby's eyes, Tubby knew that she couldn't lie to her. Tubby was ashamed of herself.

"No, I am not a princess," Tubby said sadly. "I'm not even ordinary special. I'm just an ordinary pig!"

Tubby was very sad and walked away toward home. She knew now that she was an ordinary pig. She did not want a princess friend now. She wanted just an ordinary friend. She thought that the little skunk was a princess.

"Wait!" said the little skunk. "I'm not a princess, either. I'm just an ordinary little

skunk. But I wish you would be my friend. You told me the truth and that's even better than being a princess."

"And you told me the truth, too," said Tubby. "And you're right. That is better than being a princess."

So that day

　　　　a just ordinary little pig
　　　　　　and
　　　　a just ordinary little skunk

became good friends.

But they really were *more special* than just ordinary because they always told the truth. Always telling the truth will make you *more special* than just ordinary too!

30

Are Birthday Pets Like Birthday Kids?

Someone
   came into
     my pet shop
      today.
She wanted
   a special pet
    for her
      one-year-old.
"What kind of pet?"
   I asked.
"Oh, almost any kind will do,"
   she said.

"But it must be **soft and cuddly.**
One-year-olds are **soft and cuddly**,
   you know."
Do you know one-year-olds who are
   soft and cuddly?
   Who are they?
Do you know animals who are
   soft and cuddly, too?
   What are they?

Someone came into my pet shop today.
He wanted a special pet for his two-year-
     old.
"What kind of pet?" I asked.
"Oh, almost any kind will do," he said.
  "But it must be **bouncy.**
  Two-year-olds are **bouncy,** you know."
Do you know two-year-olds who are
     bouncy?
  Who are they?
Do you know some animals who are
     bouncy, too?
  What are they?

Someone came into my pet shop today.
She wanted a special pet for her three-
    year-old.
"What kind of pet?" I asked.
"Oh, almost any kind will do," she said.
    "But it must like to **squeal and get dirty.**
    Three-year-olds like to
        squeal and get dirty, you know."
Do you know three-year-olds who like to
    squeal and get dirty?
    Who are they?
Do you know some animals who like to
    squeal and get dirty, too?
    What are they?

31

Do
Angels
Have Pets?

Do angels have pets?
 I hope that they do.
But are angel pets
 Purple, orange, or
 blue?

Do angel pets fly?
    Can they hop, skip, or walk?
And do angel pets
    Really know how to talk?

Does an angel pet sleep
    In a basket or bed?
And what is its name,
    Angelina or Fred?

Do angel pet choirs
  Like to bark, chirp, or sing?
Does an angel pet have
  At least one little wing?

Does an angel lamb *baa-aah*
  Or an angel cat *mee-ow?*
Does an angel-like pup
  Say an angel *bow-wow?*

Is angel food cake
  An angel pet treat?
I wonder what angel pets
  Really would eat.

Do angels have pets?
  I hope that they do.
If I were an angel,
  I would. Would you?

32

What Do You See When You Plant Some Seeds?

What do you see
when you plant some seeds?

Are you picking pretty flowers
  or hoeing ugly weeds?
Do you see a golden harvest
  or the sweat on your brow?
Do you see a loaf of bread
  or a dirty old plow?
Do you see Thanksgiving dinner
  or a little empty plate?
Do you see your garden grow on time
  or too little and too late?
Do you see the sun smiling
  or the raindrops fall?
Do you see abundant blessings
  or nothing much at all?
Do you see your dirty fingers
  or neatly planted rows?
Do you see empty wishes
  or hope that overflows?
What do you see
    when you plant some seeds?
Do you see a God who's far away
  or the God who meets your needs?

33

*Angel
Chores*

"It's not fair!" Gretchen grumbled. "I don't have any time to play. All day long I'm doing nothing but chores."

Mother smiled. "All day long?" she asked. "Poor Gretchen! You must be so tired. I do hope you have a little strength left. I really need that thread."

145

Gretchen smiled a little smile. She knew that Mother had not asked her to do one other thing all day long. That was her only chore so far. But she had a bad habit of grumbling when Mother asked her to do any chore. You could even call her Grumbly Gretchen.

Gretchen gave the thread to Mother. Then she sat down to play with her doll again. "There must be someone who doesn't have chores," she grumbled again. Then Gretchen saw a Sunday school paper lying on the sofa. It had a picture of an angel on it.

"Angels don't have chores," she complained. "I wish I were an angel."

Mother smiled. "Sometimes you are my little angel," she said. "But not when you grumble about chores. Anyway, how do you know that angels don't have chores?"

"Do they?" asked Gretchen.

"I don't know," said Mother. "But what if God asked angels to do some special chores for him? Do you think they would grumble?"

Gretchen giggled. She didn't think angels would grumble about anything. "What kind of chores would God ask an angel to do?" she asked.

"I don't know," said Mother. "But let's pretend:

"Angela Angel
   is sprinkling the earth
   to make
   the flowers grow.

"Andrew Angel
   is tooting his trumpet
   so the morning sunrise
   will glow.

"Allan Angel
brings in the rainbow
after the
morning rain.

"Aaron Angel
gets rid of things
that people
won't need again."

"I guess I wouldn't grumble if God asked me to do those things," said Gretchen.

"Because the chores are fun or because you love God?" Mother asked.

"Because I love God," said Gretchen. "So I guess I shouldn't grumble about your chores either, because I love you."

Gretchen really tried to stop grumbling about the few chores Mother asked her to do. Oh, she probably forgot and grumbled once in a while. But, whenever she thought about the angel chores, she tried not to grumble.

So, will you remember not to grumble, whenever you think of the angel chores?

31

That Nice Mr. Mead at Mead's Meat Market

Millie Miller shopped at Mead's Meat Market every Monday. She bought her meat for Tuesday, Wednesday, Thursday, and every other day of the week.

Why did Millie buy her meat at Mead's Meat Market? It wasn't cheaper than the meat at the supermarket. And it didn't taste any better either.

"It's that nice Mr. Mead at the meat market," said Millie. "Mr. Mead is so honest." That's what Millie told everyone who asked.

Actually Mr. Mead wasn't honest, as you

can see. Each time he put Millie's meat on the scale, he kept his finger on the scale, too. Then he pushed down a little. That made it look as if Millie's meat weighed more than it did. So Millie paid more for her meat than she should. Mr. Mead did this only with Millie. He thought he could get by with cheating her.

Poor Millie! She never looked at the scales with Mr. Mead's finger on it. She

always looked into Mr. Mead's "honest" face.

"My, my!" said Millie. "Meat is certainly expensive, isn't it?"

Mr. Mead frowned when he heard that. He knew he was cheating poor Millie. He knew Millie's meat really shouldn't cost that much. And he knew Millie could not afford to pay this much for meat.

One day Millie was buying her meat from Mr. Mead. Mr. Mead had his finger on the scale as he usually did. Suddenly Mr. Mead sneezed. When he did, his finger on the scale pushed down much harder. So the scale suddenly showed much more than it should.

"My, my!" said Millie. "That was a two-pound sneeze."

"What do you mean?" asked Mr. Mead.

"When you sneezed, the meat suddenly weighed two pounds more than it did before," said Millie. "But the meat didn't sneeze. You did! How did that happen?"

Then Mr. Mead saw that Millie was looking at the scales. He saw that Millie was looking at his finger. He quickly pulled his finger away, but it was too late. Millie had caught him!

"I've been telling everyone how honest you are," Millie told Mr. Mead. "What should I tell them now?"

Mr. Mead hung his head. He looked down at the floor. He was ashamed of himself. Millie had trusted him. She had even told people how honest he was, even while he was cheating her.

"Tell them that Mr. Mead makes things right," he said. "I'm sorry that I have cheated you. But I'm going to fix that. For the rest of this year, all your meat will be half price."

"Without your finger on the scale?" Millie asked with a smile.

"Without my finger on the scale!" said Mr. Mead.

Mr. Mead never, never put his finger on the scale again. And Millie kept buying her meat from "that nice Mr. Mead at Mead's Meat Market." She really and truly did get her meat for half price all year, too. Mr. Mead, of course, became the most honest meat man in any meat market anywhere.

35

The Best Cake Baker in the Land

Two bakers baked cakes in two bakeries. One baker baked great cakes. The other baker baked wonderful cakes. The baker who baked great cakes was humble and nice. But the baker who baked wonderful cakes was proud and boastful.

"I'm a better baker than you," boasted the baker with wonderful cakes.

"I'm the best cake baker in the land," he bragged to other shopkeepers on Bakery Street.

"No one can bake cakes better than my cakes," he gloated to people who came to buy his wonderful cakes.

People did not like to hear this baker brag. But they liked to eat the baker's cakes. They really were wonderful.

One day the Prince and a neighboring Princess decided to get married. They would have a big wedding. And they wanted a wonderful wedding cake. So they asked the proud baker who baked wonderful cakes to bake their wedding cake.

"We want you to make the most wonderful cake you have ever baked," said the Prince.

The proud baker laughed. "What else would the best baker in the land bake?" he said.

Of course that other baker who baked great cakes felt sad. He really wanted to bake the wedding cake for the Prince and Princess. But they didn't ask him.

On the day of the great wedding, the proud baker who baked wonderful cakes got up very early. He put everything in his bakery where it should be. Then he began to work. As he worked he kept saying, "I'm the best baker in all the land."

The proud baker poured the flour.

He mixed in baking powder.

He stirred in salt, sugar, and vanilla.

He broke some eggs and put them in.

He even put in some very special, secret things that I can't tell you about.

This proud baker mixed all these things together. Then he popped the layers of the cake into the oven. He baked them until they were just right.

The proud baker put the cake layers together. He put icing on the cake and fixed it just right. He stepped back and looked at his wonderful cake. "I really am the best baker in all the land," he said again.

Even the baker's kitty and puppy were getting tired of hearing him say that!

At last the baker began to decorate his wonderful wedding cake. He put a little of this here and a lot of that there. Then he put a lot of this here and a little of that there. Soon the wedding cake was really a wonderful cake. It was a masterpiece. And it was done in time for the baker to take it to the wedding. Once more the baker said, "Look at that cake! I'm the best baker in the land."

The baker picked up his wonderful cake. He walked toward the door. As he walked he said, "I'm the best baker in all the land. I'm the best baker in the land. I'm the best baker in the land."

But this best baker was thinking about himself and his cake so much that he did not watch where he was going. Suddenly he stepped on Kitty's tail. Kitty let out a terrible, blood-curdling "MEOWWWWRRRR" and jumped into the air. Kitty landed on Puppy. Her claws dug into Puppy's nose.

Puppy let out a blood-curdling "YIIIIIIP" and leaped toward Kitty. Kitty tried to get away. The only place she could climb was up the baker's trousers. She leaped to the top of the wonderful cake. Puppy leaped after her.

"Plop!" went the wonderful cake to the floor.

"Plop!" went the proud baker beside his wonderful cake, which wasn't so wonderful now.

The proud baker looked at his cake. What a mess it was! Kitty was still clinging to one side, with icing dripping from her claws. Puppy was on another layer of cake, still growling at Kitty.

The proud baker looked very sad now. He really wasn't proud now. He was in BIG trouble and he knew it. There would be no wonderful cake at the wedding. People would be very angry. He would not be the best baker in the land. No one would want to buy his cakes any more.

"What will I do? What can I do?" asked the proud baker. This proud baker was feeling quite humble.

"I must go and tell the Prince and Princess and their wedding guests what happened," the baker said to himself. "I must go now." So he started to walk down Bakery Street.

On the way the baker passed the other bakery. The baker who baked great cakes was busily working inside. "Where are you going?" he asked the proud baker.

"To the wedding," said the sad baker.

"But where is your cake?" asked the baker in the bakery shop.

Then the sad baker told his sad story.

"Come in here," said the baker in the bakery shop. There on the table was a beautiful wedding cake.

"I wanted to bake the wedding cake for the Prince and Princess," said the baker in the bakery. "But I knew they asked you. So I baked this cake and pretended it was for them. Take it. You can pretend that you made it."

"I will gladly take it," said the other baker. "But only if you come with me. I want to tell the Prince and Princess and all their friends that you are the best baker in the land."

Saving
Time

36
My
Piggy

Sarah was a spender. She liked to spend every penny someone gave her. She also liked to spend every penny she earned. Sarah couldn't wait to spend it for something special. She spent her money as soon as she got it.

"Why don't you save some of your money," said Mother. "When you get enough, you can spend it for something special."

Sarah tried that two or three times. But every time she looked at her money, she wanted to spend it.

"I have an idea," said Mother. "Why not

160

spend some of your money for a piggy bank? You can save your money in it. You won't see it. So you won't want to spend it."

Sarah thought that was a good idea. So she spent some money for a piggy bank. Mother helped her buy it. Sarah thought it was the cutest little piggy in all the world.

It was fun to save money in this cute piggy bank. Each time Sarah put money into the piggy, she talked to it. She pretended the piggy could hear her.

"You're helping me save my money, you know," Sarah told the piggy one day.

"You're the cutest piggy I've ever seen," Sarah told the piggy another day.

"I like having you in my room," Sarah told the piggy still another day.

Each day Sarah talked to her piggy bank. Each time she put money into it, she told it how cute it was, or how much she liked it.

Each day Sarah told her mother how much she liked this cute piggy bank. At first she called it "that piggy bank." Then she called it "my piggy bank." Then she began to call it "My Piggy!"

Sarah saved every penny she earned. She saved every penny someone gave her. That's so she could talk to Piggy when she put money into him. Saving was such fun now.

One day Sarah went to Amy's birthday party. You should see the beautiful doll Amy got for her birthday! Sarah wanted a doll like that. She was sure that she must have enough in Piggy to buy her doll.

After Amy's birthday party, Sarah ran home as fast as she could. She found a hammer and ran to her room. She would smash that piggy bank and get the money for the doll.

Then Sarah looked at her piggy bank. It wasn't "that piggy bank." It was "My Piggy." A tear came to Sarah's eyes. She was almost sure that she saw a tear in Piggy's eyes, too.

Sarah put the hammer away. "I won't smash Piggy for any old doll," she said.

The next day Sarah went to Sunday school. The teacher told Sarah and her class about a missionary family their church supported. They had a little girl Sarah's age. Their house had just burned. They lost everything they had. If people didn't help them, they would have to come home. They would have to stop working for Jesus in that place until they could get a new house.

"We're going to take an offering next Sunday," said the teacher. "If you want to help Jesus do his work, this is a good place to give some of your money."

On the way home, Sarah thought about this missionary family. She thought about the girl her age.

"I want to give the money I have in My Piggy," she said. "That's much more important than buying a doll."

When she came home, Sarah got the hammer again. She would simply HAVE to break Piggy open for Jesus.

But when Sarah looked at her Piggy she began to cry. Piggy had a tear, too.

But Sarah lifted the hammer. "I MUST get my money out for Jesus," she said. Sarah lifted the hammer three times. Each time she said, "I MUST get my money out for Jesus." But each time she put the hammer down. She could not break her Piggy.

Sarah ran to Mother as fast as she could go. She was crying so much she thought her heart would break.

"What should I do?" she begged.

"About what?" asked Mother.

Sarah told Mother about wanting to give her money to Jesus. She was even willing to break her Piggy for Jesus. But it was SO hard to do it.

"That's easy," said Mother. "Why don't you use the key that came with the bank? Or did I forget to tell you about the key?"

Sarah stared at Mother. She threw her arms around Mother and cried some more.

"Oh, thank you, thank you, thank you," Sarah said. She probably said "thank you" a dozen times.

If you ever want to see a happy Sarah, you should have seen Sarah opening Piggy's tummy with the key Mother gave her. Sarah had a smile as big as the sun. She was sure that Piggy had a smile just as big, too.

37

King Kent of Kent's Kingdom

Kent liked to play after he came home from school. Sometimes he liked to play outside. Sometimes he liked to play inside. On rainy days he liked to play inside more than outside. Do you?

On this rainy day Kent sat down with his crayons, scissors, paper, and glue. He began to cut and color and glue.

"You're so busy," said Mother. "What are you making?"

"I'm making a surprise," said Kent. "You'll be proud of me when you see it."

"I'm always proud of you," said Mother. "But this sounds quite special."

"Oh, it is!" said Kent. "When I finish this, I will be a very important person."

"It sounds like a very important activity," said Mother. "I can hardly wait to see it."

Kent was busy for a long time. At last he called for Mother.

"Come and see my surprise," he said.

Mother hurried to see Kent's surprise. There was Kent, still holding his scissors and glue. Crayons stuck out of his back pocket with his sling. Paper and crayons were all over the floor.

But, most important, Kent wore a big smile. He also wore a paper crown he had made.

"I'm a king!" said Kent. "I'm King Kent of Kent's Kingdom!"

"That's exciting," said Mother. "You will make a good king. But what do you want to do as king?"

Kent was quiet for a moment. "Do kings have to do something?" he asked. "I thought they were just kings."

Mother said, "Good kings do good things. Bad kings do bad things. But they all do some things."

"I want good things in my kingdom," said Kent. "Kent's Kingdom will be a good place. But can't I just BE good? Do I have to DO good things?"

Mother smiled. "When you're good, you

do good things," she said. "When you do good things, you show that you are good."

"Then I guess I want to BE good and DO good things," said King Kent. "Is wearing a crown doing something good? Must I do something more?"

"A king isn't a king because he wears a crown," said Mother. "A king wears a crown because he is first a king. If you want to be a king, you must do things good kings do."

"Like what?" asked King Kent.

"Kingly kindness is a good start," said Mother. "Do kind things for your subjects."

King Kent laughed. "Who are my subjects?" he asked.

"How about Kitty and Puppy?" asked Mother.

"I'll do kind things for them," said King Kent. "I'll love them, too."

"That's fit for a king," said Mother. "A good king should love his subjects. And he will help take care of his subjects."

"Sounds like I have some royal work to do," said King Kent. "It is time to feed Kitty and Puppy. So I'll wear my crown while I feed my subjects."

"When you're through, you can join us for a palace banquet," said Mother. "Dinner is almost ready. But do kings help their mothers wash and dry dishes after the palace banquet?"

"This king will," said Kent. "I'll even wear my crown. Helping my mother is kingly work, you know!"

Wouldn't you like to have a picture of King Kent wearing his crown while he helped mother with the dishes? Father took one. He might show it to you some time.

38

*What's
for
Dinner?*

Are chocolate eggs
for
breakfast,

Or
cornflakes
made
for
lunch?

Do most of us
start out the day
With birthday cake
and punch?

Would Puppy like a cherry pie,
And would you want his bone?
Would you enjoy a piggy's grain,
And he your ice-cream cone?

Would Teddy Bear sit in a chair
And feast on candy cane?
And would a cow begin right now
A diet of chow mein?

Is lemonade that's freshly made
The thing for every critter?
And would you pay to buy some hay
For baby's baby-sitter?

You wouldn't be exactly glad
For dinner at the zoo.
So you'll be glad to know that God
Has planned good foods for you.

39

The Queen of Clean

When it was time for Doreene to help with the dishes, she began to complain. "Why do we have to rinse and wash and scrub and dry all these old dishes?" she moaned.

When Mother asked Doreene to help dust the furniture, she griped about that. When it was Doreene's time to clean her room, she had a few things to say about that, too.

When it was time to help mother wash the clothes, Doreene grumbled about that. "Just think," she said, "if we wore all these

clothes twice as long before washing, we would wash half as much."

"Your math is great," said Father. "But the Queen of Clean wouldn't rule a kingdom like that!"

"Who is she?" Doreene asked. She had a little half-smile when she asked. She knew Father would tell a story, which he did. This is Father's story:

Once upon a time, the Countess of Complaining complained about almost everything. That's why she was the Countess of Complaining. But she complained most about washing and drying dishes, washing clothes, keeping her room clean, and dusting the furniture.

One day the Countess of Complaining had a big royal party. She invited all her favorite royal guests.

The Duke of Dust arrived first. He came as soon as the Countess complained about dusting furniture. The Duke had a big bag of dust with him. He sprinkled it over all the furniture in the palace.

The Countess didn't care. "Someone else will clean it up," she thought. She never thought about who that "someone else" would be.

176

The Duchess of Dirty Dishes arrived next. She came as soon as the Countess complained about rinsing, washing, and drying dirty dishes. You should have seen all the dirty dishes the Duchess had with her.

The Countess was sure that the Duchess must have had a banquet of garbage. These were not just dirty dishes. They were yukky, sticky, gooey, dirty dishes. Even the pigs would have been ashamed of them! The Duchess piled all her dirty dishes in the sink. They reached to the ceiling of the palace. Mustard, ketchup, syrup, and leftovers dripped from the dishes.

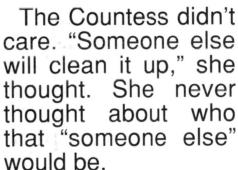

The Countess didn't care. "Someone else will clean it up," she thought. She never thought about who that "someone else" would be.

The Marquis of Mud was next. He came when the Countess complained that she always had to take off her muddy shoes at the door. Of course the Marquis didn't do that. He had so much mud on his shoes that he could hardly walk. He took a tour of the palace. There was a mile of mud everywhere.

The Countess didn't care. "Someone else will clean it up," she thought. She never thought about who that "someone else" would be.

Prince Pig Sty came next. He arrived when the Countess complained about washing and ironing clothes. His clothes looked as if he had just come from a long game of football with the pigs. They were filthy. The Countess was sure he had not washed his clothes in a month of Sundays. When he came in, Prince Pig Sty sat in every pretty chair he could find. He loved to see the dirty streaks that he left behind.

The Countess didn't care. "Someone else will clean it up," she thought. She never thought about who that "someone else" would be.

Baron La Mold left moldy pieces of bread in the corners of the palace. General Germs coughed and sneezed at everyone he could find. Admiral Hornblower left a trail of dirty tissues on the floor. Major Mess threw toys and junk everywhere.

The Countess didn't care. "Someone else will clean it up," she thought. She never thought about who that "someone else" would be.

At last the party was over. The royal guests all went home. The Countess went to bed and slept very well because she was sure that "someone else will clean up all the mess" while she slept.

But the next morning the Countess was surprised. Dirty food still dripped from the dishes. Dust still covered all the furniture. There was still a mile of mud throughout the palace. Everywhere she looked she saw dirty tissues, toys, and junk. No one else had cleaned it up.

Suddenly the Countess remembered. In real life, Mother cleaned up these things when she complained and didn't help. But Mother didn't live in this Pretend Palace!

Eight hundred and eighty-eight days later, the Countess was just cleaning up the last of the mess. Suddenly there was a knock on the door. When she opened the door, there were all her royal friends—the Duke of Dust, the Duchess of Dirty Dishes, the Marquis of Mud, Baron La Mold, Prince Pig Sty, General Germs, Admiral Hornblower, and Major Mess. They wanted another party.

"Go away and never come back," said the Countess. "You're not wanted!"

"But you always wanted us before," they said.

"That's when I was the Countess of Complaining," she said. "Now I'm the Queen of Clean. From now on, I want to have the cleanest castle in the kingdom."

When Father finished his story, Doreene smiled. "I guess I want to be the Queen of Clean instead of the Countess of Complaining," she said. "Doreene, the Queen of Clean! That sounds good. I think Mother will like to hear my new title."

From that time on, whenever Doreene thought about complaining, she remembered the royal guests and the eight hundred and eighty-eight days of cleaning up their mess. Whenever there was anything to be cleaned, Doreene became Mother's special helper.

"The Queen of Clean at your service!" she would always say with a smile. Then the Queen of Clean and Mother would have a mess cleaned up in less than eight hundred and eighty-eight seconds!

40

Moving Day

Moving day, please go away,
And don't come back another day.
I really do not want to go
To a strange home that I don't know.
I fear my friendships all will end,
And I'll go there without a friend.

I'm filled with fear, I cry at night,
I'm scared that things won't work out
    right.
I really do not want to go
To a strange home that I don't know.
I fear my friendships all will end,
And I'll go there without a friend.

I'll leave friends here who care for me,
But will I find new friends friendly?
I really do not want to go
To a strange home that I don't know.
I fear my friendships all will end,
And I'll go there without a friend.

Will kids at school refuse to play?
Will they have nasty things to say?
I really do not want to go
To a strange home that I don't know.
I fear my friendships all will end,
And I'll go there without a friend.

But then last night I learned in prayer
My Best Friend is already there.

Moving day, don't go away,
I'm ready now, please come today.
I know I'm ready now to go
To that strange home that I don't know.
I've learned new friendships all begin
Not with new kids, but from within!

Because last night I learned in prayer
My Best Friend is already there.

41

What's So Special About a Baby?

What's so special about a baby?

A baby
can't say
one word
can't wash
one dish
can't feed
one pet

But a baby is very, very special. Why?

Is it because a baby
doesn't say one mean word,
doesn't break one dish, or
doesn't tease one pet?
No, that's not what makes a baby special.

What's so special about a baby?

A baby
can't cook one meal
can't play ball
can't ride a bike

But a baby is very, very special. Why?

Is it because a baby
doesn't burn the toast,
doesn't throw a ball through the window,
    or
doesn't fall from a bike and skin her
    knee?
No, that's not what makes a baby spe-
    cial.

What's so special about a baby?

A baby
can't drive a car
can't play with brothers and sisters
can't climb stairs

But a baby is very, very special. Why?

Is it because a baby
doesn't get a speeding ticket,
doesn't fight with brothers and sisters,
or
doesn't fall down stairs?
No, that's not what makes a baby
special.

If a baby doesn't give us trouble
because he can't get into trouble,
And doesn't argue
because she can't talk,

And doesn't go to bad places
  because he can't walk,
And doesn't fall
  because she can't stand up,
Does that make a baby special?
No, these are not the things that make a
  baby special.

What's so special about a baby?
A baby is very, very special because:

When I see our newborn baby,
  I remember our Creator.
When I see our baby's smile,
  I remember God is love.
When I see how helpless baby is,
  I remember God's watchcare.
When I see our baby's little feet,
  I remember to follow Jesus.
When I see our baby's tiny fingers,
  I remember the joy of serving Jesus.
When I see our baby's soft lips,
  I remember to tell others about Jesus.
When I hear our baby coo,
  I remember to praise our Lord.
When I see our baby's softness,
  I remember God's compassion.
When I see our baby drinking milk,
  I remember God provides.
When I see our baby in our arms,
  I remember God holds us tight.

When I see our baby awake each morn-
  ing,
  I remember God was with me through
  the night.
When I see our baby go to sleep,
  I remember God is with us always.
When I see our baby grow,
  I remember God is faithful.

Thank you, Lord, for showing us more
  about you,
  as we see our little baby.

42

*Take
a
Bow*

"How did you like Diane's piano recital, Denny?" Mother asked.

"It was okay," said Denny. "She did a good job with her piece. But why did people clap for the piano players? Why did the piano players bow when they did?"

"When Father and I go to musical concerts, people clap for the musicians there, too," said Mother. "Then the musicians bow. Sometimes the people clap for a long time."

"Why?" asked Denny.

"We clap because we like what they did

for us," said Mother. "We clap to say 'thank you.' They bow to say 'you're welcome.'"

"But you don't clap for me when I do something special," said Denny. "If you did, I'd take a bow, too!"

"Would you like that?" said Mother.

"That would be fun!" said Denny.

"We'll talk about it when Father comes home," said Mother.

Father smiled when Denny told him about clapping and taking a bow. Father and Mother said they would try it. Diane thought it was silly.

Denny was so happy to hear this. At last his family would show they appreciated him.

But Denny had almost forgotten about their little talk when he and Diane fed Puppy and Kitty. When they finished, Mother and Father clapped and cheered for Denny.

"Take a bow, Denny," said Father.

Denny bowed. He felt a little silly, though. After all, he had just done his chores.

"Wait a minute!" said Diane. "I fed Puppy and Kitty, too."

"We'll clap for you, if you want us to," said Father.

"I'd feel absolutely stupid," said Diane. "Feeding Puppy and Kitty is part of our chores. Don't clap for me."

As soon as Denny and Diane had helped Mother set the table, Mother and Father clapped their hands.

"Yeah, Denny!" they shouted. Father even gave a long whistle.

"Diane helped, too," he said, sheepishly.

"She doesn't want us to clap for her, Denny," said Father. "Take a bow."

Denny gave a little halfhearted bow. He wasn't so sure this really was fun. He really did feel silly.

After dinner, Mother and Father jumped up from the table. They began to clap and cheer for Denny.

"What's that for?" asked Denny. "I didn't do anything."

"You ate dinner," said Mother. "Yeah, Denny. Take a bow."

Denny started to get up from the table to take a bow. But he couldn't do it.

"I feel stupid!" he said. "I don't want clapping for eating dinner."

"How about for helping with dishes?" asked Mother. "Or cleaning up your room or going to school or getting good grades?"

"I don't want you to clap for me for any of these things," said Denny. "I *should* go to school, get good grades, clean up my room, feed our pets, help set the table, and eat my dinner."

"Then what should we clap for?" asked Mother.

"Nothing," said Denny. "But I do want to take a bow." So Denny bowed.

"What for?" asked Father.

"That's my way of saying 'thank you' to my parents for all they do for me," he said. "I never clap for all the things you do for me, so I'll take a bow."

Would you like to clap your hands or take a bow to your parents for all they do for you? Or would you rather just say "thanks"?

43

*Full Heart
and
Empty Bank*

Penny was sad. She wanted to buy something special for each person in her family. But she had no money. Her piggy bank was empty.

"I wish I could buy that beautiful dress for Mother," said Penny. "But I don't have one dollar." Penny shook her piggy bank. There wasn't one dollar in it.

"I wish I could buy that sweater Father wants," said Penny. "But I don't have one quarter." Penny shook her piggy bank. There wasn't one quarter in it.

"I wish I could buy that beautiful doll for my little sister," said Penny. "But I don't

have one nickel." Penny shook her piggy
bank. There wasn't one nickel in it.

"I wish I could buy that beautiful bike for
my big brother," said Penny. "But I don't

have one dime." Penny shook her piggy bank. There wasn't one dime in it.

Penny shook her piggy bank again. She knew what she would hear. There was nothing in it, not even one penny. She wished she could hear even one little penny rattling around inside. But she didn't. It was empty.

Poor Penny! Her heart was full, but her bank was empty.

Penny sighed.

Then Penny had an idea. "I can't BUY each of my family members something special," she said. "But maybe I can DO something special for each one."

Penny ran to find Mother. She was getting ready to wash the dinner dishes.

"Mother, Mother," said Penny, "I have a wonderful gift for you."

Mother smiled. She knew that Penny did not have even one penny to buy a wonderful gift.

"I'm going to wash and dry all the dinner dishes," said Penny. "And you are going to sit down and read."

Mother smiled. "All by yourself?" asked Mother. "Are you sure?"

Penny looked so happy that Mother knew she was sure.

When Penny finished the dishes, she ran

to find Father. He was getting ready to sweep the garage.

"Guess what!" said Penny. "I have a wonderful gift for you."

Father smiled. He knew that Penny did not have even one penny to buy a wonderful gift.

"I'm going to sweep the garage for you," said Penny. "And you are going to sit down and read."

Father smiled. "All by yourself?" he asked. "Are you sure?"

Penny looked so happy that Father knew she was sure.

When Penny finished sweeping the garage, she ran to find her big brother. He was getting ready to feed Puppy and Kitty.

"Guess what?" said Penny. "I have a wonderful gift for you."

Penny's big brother smiled. He knew that Penny did not have even one penny to buy a wonderful gift.

"I'm going to feed Puppy and Kitty for you," said Penny. "And you are going to play with your toys."

Penny's big brother smiled. "All by yourself?" he asked. "Are you sure?"

Penny looked so happy that her big brother knew she was sure.

When Penny finished feeding Puppy and

Kitty, she ran to find her little sister. She was getting ready to play all by herself.

"Guess what?" said Penny. "I have a wonderful gift for you."

Penny's little sister smiled. She knew that Penny did not have even one penny to buy a wonderful gift.

"I'm going to play with you," said Penny.

"Are you sure?" asked Penny's little sister. She knew that it wasn't much fun for big sisters to play little-sister stuff with their little sisters.

Penny looked so happy that her little sister knew she was sure.

Later that evening, Penny walked into the living room. There were four smiling people, waiting for her.

"Guess what!" said Penny's little sister.

"We have a wonderful gift for you," said Penny's big brother.

"A big hug," said Father.

"For a wonderful girl," said Mother.

So Penny had four big hugs, one from Mother, one from Father, one from her big brother, and one from her little sister.

Penny didn't even bother to shake her empty piggy bank. She thought she was the richest girl in all the world.

What do you think?

44

*Mike
the
Knight*

"Who is this fierce-looking knight?" asked Father.

"I'm Mike the Mighty Knight," said Mike.

Mike the Knight looked something like a real knight. He had a sword, a helmet, and a shield. He pretended that his shirt was armor.

"I'm ready to fight," said Mike.

"Whom do you want to fight?" asked Dad.

"I want to fight those guys at school who made fun of me," said Mike.

"I'm sorry they did that," said Father. "Why did they make fun of you?"

"Because I told them that I love Jesus,"

said Mike. "And because I told them that I read my Bible and pray. They also want me to do some things that would not please Jesus."

Father smiled. "Mike the Knight, there are some people like that where I work," he said. "They make fun of me because I love Jesus. They tease me because I read my Bible and pray. They think I should do some of the bad things they do."

"After I fight those guys at school, I'll come and fight those guys at your work," said Mike.

Father smiled. "With your sword?" he asked. "What do you want to do to your guys and my guys?"

"I'll chop them with my sword," said Mike.

"That's sounds rough," said Father. "Do you really want to hurt them?"

Mike hadn't thought about that. He really didn't want to hurt anyone with his sword. He just wanted to stop the teasing. He didn't want to do the bad things his friends did. But he didn't want to chop anyone either.

"You need a different sword to fight your friends," said Father.

"But this is a genuine, trusty, guaranteed knight's sword," said Mike. "It's the best!"

"I'm sure it's the best sword to hurt people," said Father. "But you're not going to

203

win your battle for Jesus by chopping people with that kind of sword. There is a special sword to help you win Jesus' battles."

Mike looked puzzled. "Can I buy one?" he asked. "Does it cost a lot of money?"

"You already have one," said Father.

"I do?" asked Mike. He really looked puzzled now. "What is it? Where is it?"

"Come with me, Mike the Mighty Knight," said Father. Mike and Father went to Mike's room. Father picked up Mike's Bible.

"Here it is!" said Father.

"But . . . but that's not a sword," said Mike. "That's just my Bible."

"It doesn't look like a sword," said Father. "But it is."

Father opened Mike's Bible and read from Ephesians 6:11–17.

"Put on the whole armor of God," Father read. Then Father read about God's special sword, his Word, the Bible.

"Does the Bible really say that?" asked Mike the Knight. "Does the Bible really say that it is God's special sword?"

"Yes, it does," said Father. "Ordinary knights wear ordinary swords. They chop people with them. But Christians are God's special knights. We use God's special sword, the Bible, to help Jesus."

Mike the Knight put down his knight's

sword. He picked up God's sword, his Bible.

"I'm ready to change swords," he said. "But how do I use it as a sword?"

"You don't chop people with it," said Father. "You share it with others, the way Jesus did when he was tempted."

Father read the story in Matthew 4:1–11 about the devil tempting Jesus. "Every time the devil tempted Jesus, he answered him with a Bible verse," said Father. "Each Bible verse was like a sword jabbing the devil. But God does the jabbing, we don't!"

"So when my friends tempt me to do something wrong, I should share a Bible verse with them?" asked Mike the Knight.

"Try it!" said Father. "That's what I do with my friends at work. It works."

"I will," said Mike. "I want to have my sword ready, so I'm going to start memorizing some Bible verses."

Would you like to get your sword ready, too?

45

What Will You Say?

What will you say
   if you find
      a dollar?
Will you want a gold chain
   to hang around
      your collar?

What will you say
   if you find
      a pearl?
Will you feel like
      a queen,
         a princess, or
            an earl?

What will you say
  if you find a new friend?
Do you have something special
  that you hope will never end?

What will you say
  when your family gets together?
Will you feel you can face
  any storm in any weather?

What will you say
  when God says, "I love you"?
Will you love and follow him
  in everything you do?

A pearl may be special
  and a dollar's special, too.
But they simply can't compare
  when you see what God gives you.

**Reading
Time**

46
Why?

Tell me why
  my heart wants playtime
  but my hands
    must do the chores.

Tell me why
  it's often raining
  when I want
    to play outdoors.

Tell me why
  I'm wide awake
  when it's time
    to go to bed.

Tell me why
I feel so sleepy
when I should
wake up instead.

Tell me why
I don't like spinach
and the stuff that
helps me grow.

Tell me why
  I feast on candy
  and other things
    that are no no.

Tell me why
  I want to go
  when I know
    that I should stay.

Tell me why
  I'm told to shush
  when I have
    so much to say.

Tell me why
  I'm looking back,
  when I should
    look on ahead.

Tell me why
  I'm looking DOWN at me
  when I should
    look UP to God
      instead!

47

*Why
Do I Say
No?*

When Mother knows what's good for me,
    Why do I say no?
When Father says, "This way is best,"
    Why don't I want to go?

When teacher tries to help me learn,
    Why do I refuse?
When choosing chores will help me grow,
    Why don't I choose to choose?

When Jesus walks ahead of me,
    And gives me all I need,
Or when he wants to guide my life,
    Why don't I let him lead?

I think I know what I should do,
When tempted to say no.
I'll ask the Lord what he would do,
And that's the way I'll go.

48

What Should I Say to God?

"Bedtime, Barry!" Mother called.

"That means it's time to pray," said Barry. "Why do I have to pray every night before I go to bed?"

"You don't have to," said Mother. "But don't you want to?"

"I guess so," said Barry. "But sometimes I don't know what to say to God."

Mother smiled. "Most people wonder what they should say to God," she said. "They're afraid they aren't saying the right words."

"I guess I should just keep asking him for

things," said Barry. "Isn't that what we should do when we pray?"

"You can ask him for what you want," said Mother. "Or you can ask him for what is best for you."

Barry thought about that. "I . . . I guess I've really been asking for what I want," he said. "Maybe some of these things aren't so good for me. Maybe God really doesn't want me to have every one of them."

"I'm glad to hear you say that," said Mother. "Many of my friends haven't figured that out yet. They pray, 'Dear God, gimme what I want.' That's a GIMME PRAYER."

Barry laughed. "What kinds of prayers should I pray?" he asked.

"Let's start with a THANK-YOU PRAYER," said Mother. "Thank God for good things he has given you."

"I could pray an hour about that," said Barry. "What else?"

"How about a PRAISE-YOU PRAYER?" said Mother. "Tell God how glad you are for the kind of person God is. Praise him for his love. Praise him for his kindness. Praise him for His goodness. You could think of a dozen good things about God."

"I guess I could pray an hour about that, too," said Barry. "Is there another kind of prayer I should remember?"

"I don't have to tell you much about a HELP-ME PRAYER," said Mother. "When you need help, I know you will ask God to help you. But how about an I-GIVE-YOU PRAYER? You can talk with God about what you will give Him."

Barry was quiet when Mother said that. "I guess I'm always asking God for so much I never tell him what I want to give him," he said. "I want to give him some of my money. But what else?"

"You can sing well," said Mother. "That's called a talent. You can give that to God. So now you have two things—money and talents. But what is the most important gift you can give God?"

Barry smiled. "I know!" he said. "I can give him myself."

"God would rather have that special gift than all the money you could give," she said.

"Prayer time," said Barry. "I have lots and lots of things to pray about tonight."

49

*What
Do You
Want?*

If God would give
   you anything,
What would
   you ask today?
If God would share
   while you're at prayer,
What would
   you want to pray?

218

Would you become a movie star,
  Or quarterback a team?
Would you request a pirate chest,
  A truckload of ice cream?

A castle might be very nice,
  A red sports car or two.
What if God made a great parade,
  Or a circus just for you?

A million dollars would be great,
  A million more is greater.
How about the gold to fill the hold,
  Of a twenty-mile-long freighter?

If you could be the smartest kid,
  You'd know that you would pass.
You'd spend all day at fun and play,
  And still be first in class.

If God would give you anything,
  Would these things pass the test?
Or could he pour out something more,
  To help you have his best?

I'd think you'd give up anything,
  To know that God loves you.
So when you pray, perhaps you'll say,
  You'll give him your love, too.

50

*I
Don't
Know
Why*

I don't know why it happens,
    When I reach out for a crown,
When I think
        that I deserve
        the prize,
The world
        turns
            upside
            down.

I don't know why it happens,
When I think that I am best,
When I think that I can prove it,
Something puts me to the test.

I don't know why it happens,
When I think I'm very wise,
And I think I know the answer,
Something cuts me down to size.

I don't know why it happens,
When I'm proud of what I've done,
And I want to show off all my works,
That I'm forced to show off none.

Wait! I do know why it happens!
I remember it today!
I find that things don't turn out right,
When I forget to pray!

51

The Worrier

Wilda was a worrier. She worried about almost everything. Sometimes she worried because she was a worrier.

"How will I ever pay my bills?" Wilda would ask. Each bill seemed bigger than the last bill. Each time Wilda wrote a check it seemed as if the checkbook was shrinking. She could almost see it disappear.

"I'll never have enough money to fix the car and pay the rent," Wilda worried.

Somehow Wilda always seemed to have enough money. She always was able to pay her bills. Sometimes they were a little late. But she did pay them.

Wilda worried about getting sick. "I just know I'll get some terrible disease," Wilda worried. "I'll get in the hospital. Then I won't be able to pay for it."

Sometimes Wilda worried that she would not have enough to eat. Sometimes she worried that she would not sleep. Sometimes she was so worried that she couldn't sleep.

"Why do I worry so much?" Wilda wondered.

"Because you think you have to do everything," said a friend. "Let God help you. If you really trust him, you won't worry so much."

But Wilda worried that God would not help her. She worried that she could not trust God if he didn't help her.

One day Wilda was whomping up a good worry storm. She wasn't even thinking about what God could do.

Wilda was watching her kitty as she worried. Kitty slept a little, yawned, blinked her eyes, then slept some more.

"I wish I could be like you," said Wilda the Worrier. "You don't worry about anything. Why?"

The more Wilda thought about Kitty, the more she realized how different she and

Kitty were. Wilda worried about everything. Kitty worried about nothing.

"Of course you don't have to worry," Wilda said to Kitty. "You always have food to eat."

Then Wilda thought about what she had said. "I guess I always have food to eat, too," she said.

"You don't worry because you always have our warm home to live in," Wilda said to Kitty.

Then Wilda thought about what she had said. "I guess I always have our warm home to live in, too," she said.

"But you always have your warm coat," Wilda complained to Kitty.

Then Wilda thought about what she had said. "I guess I always have warm clothes, too," she said.

"But you have. . . ." Wilda started to say. She stopped. She couldn't think of one good thing that Kitty had that she didn't have.

Then Wilda began counting all her blessings. She began to write a list of all the special things she had. Kitty didn't have half as many things as Wilda.

"I have twice as much as Kitty," said Wilda. "I even have a hundred times more than Kitty. If that cat doesn't worry, why should I?"

Then Wilda softly prayed, "Dear God, thank you for all I have. Help me trust you and thank you for what I have, instead of worrying about what I don't have. Amen."

Each time Wilda started to worry, she looked at Kitty. Then she thanked God for each of her blessings. She named each blessing as she thanked God for it.

Wilda became less and less Wilda the Worrier. More and more she became Wilda the Pray-er. She also became Wilda the Blessing Counter. She counted her blessings so many times that she could list them all for you.

The next time you are tempted to worry, remember Wilda. Stop! Count your blessings! Thank God for each one. Then watch your worries shrink.

52

A
Little Lamb
Whispered

A little lamb whispered
  softly today,
"Please be my shepherd,
  show me your way.
But before you lead,
  I hope that you go,
Where
  your
    Shepherd
     leads
  and
    helps
     you
      to
       grow."

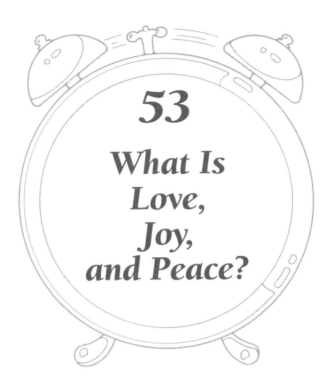

53

*What Is
Love,
Joy,
and Peace?*

What is love?
Do you know?

My mother says,
"It's
  changing
    dirty
      diapers
And
  scrubbing
  dirty
    toes.

It's working hard without reward."
Do you suppose she knows?

What is joy?
Do you know?

My mother says,
"It's more than being happy,
By getting lots of things.
It's the deep-down satisfaction
That serving Jesus brings."

What is peace?
Do you know?

My mother says,
"It's more than being quiet,
Away from girls and boys.
It's pleasing God and building kids,
With lots of family noise."

54

Connie's Complaints

"Why do I have to look so ugly with these old curlers tonight?" asked Connie.

"So you can look beautiful without them tomorrow," said Mother.

"Why can't I look beautiful without them tonight *and* tomorrow?" asked Connie.

"Does your hair curl all by itself?" Mother asked.

"No," said Connie.

"Do you want to get up early so I can curl it with a curling iron in the morning?"

"No."

"Do you want to go to school with your hair not curled?"

SCALES

"No."

"Do you know some other way to curl your hair?"

Connie thought a while. She didn't know of any other way to have curly hair. And she did want curly hair.

"Why didn't you let me eat that candy tonight?" Connie grumbled.

Mother smiled.

"How many pieces did I let you eat?" she asked.

"Two."

"How many did you want to eat?"

"Hundreds."

"How much do you think you and I would weigh if we ate hundreds of pieces of candy?"

Connie frowned. She didn't even want to think about that.

"Why do I always have to take a bath with that old soapy water," Connie complained.

"So you will keep clean," said Mother. "If you don't keep clean, you can get germs. Your friends may also sit on the other side of the room."

This time Connie smiled. She knew what Mother meant. But Connie was on a roll with her complaints.

"Why do I have to scrub my pretty teeth with that old toothbrush?" Connie groaned.

"So your pretty white teeth won't get yellow fur all over them," said Mother. "You don't want to see yellow fur all over your teeth, do you?"

"Yuk!" said Connie.

"Also, if you don't brush your teeth, they get cavities easily," said Mother. "Do you like it when the dentist drills holes in your teeth to fill them?"

"Ouch!" said Connie.

But Connie was still grumbling and complaining about curlers, candy, soap, and toothbrushes when she went to sleep. It just didn't seem fair that she had to mess around with all those things.

That night Connie dreamed a strange dream. She threw all her curlers, bath soap, and toothbrushes in the garbage. She was so happy to throw all that junk away. She wouldn't have to mess with those things any more.

Then Connie sat down with the biggest

box of chocolates that you've ever seen. It was as big as her bed. She ate and ate and ate. She ate the whole thing!

You would think that Connie would brush her teeth after eating so many chocolates. But she didn't. And she didn't take a soapy bath or curl her hair either.

In her dream Connie saw herself getting bigger and bigger. She had to run from her room so she could get through her bedroom door. When she looked in the mirror in the hallway, she looked like a big Connie-shaped balloon. Then she saw that her hair was long and stringy. She looked at her teeth. They had yellow fur on them.

Connie dreamed that she was suddenly at school. But her friends laughed at her because she was a Connie-shaped balloon with stringy hair and yellow furry teeth.

Her friends also sat on the other side of the room because she hadn't bathed with soapy water. Connie began to cry. She was ashamed to be a Connie-shaped balloon with stringy hair and furry yellow teeth. She was ashamed that kids wanted to sit on the other side of the room.

Connie cried all the way home. She tried to get into the house, but she couldn't get through the door. Connie pounded on the door and screamed for Mother.

Suddenly Connie felt a warm hand touch her forehead. "Bad dream?" a soft voice asked.

Connie looked up. She was in her bed in her room. Mother was smiling at her. She wasn't a big Connie-shaped balloon with stringy hair and yellow furry teeth. She was little. Her teeth still felt minty from brushing. But she did have curlers in her hair.

"I'm glad for curlers and toothbrushes and toothpaste and soapy bathwater," Connie whispered to Mother. "And I'm glad you didn't let me eat all the candy I wanted."

"I'm glad that you're glad," said Mother. "And I know you'll still be glad in the morning." And she was!

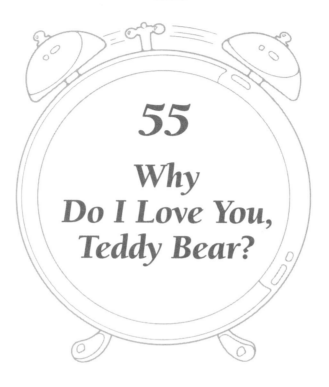

55

*Why
Do I Love You,
Teddy Bear?*

You ask me
  why I love you,
  Teddy Bear?
I'll tell you
  if you promise not to tell
  anyone else.
Okay?

I love you
  because you never
  argue or fight with me.
You'll never do that,
  will you?

I love you
   because you never say
   mean things about me
   to your friends.
I wish I could say that
   about my
   other friends.

I love you
   because you're always there
   when I need a friend.
You always will be,
   won't you?

I love you
  because you always smile
  at me.
You'll never frown
  or look angry at me,
  will you?

I love you
  because you've never
  run away from me.
You'll always be there with me,
  won't you?

I love you
  because you're huggable.
When I need someone to hug,
  you comfort me.

I love you
  because you watch over me
  all night while I'm asleep.
You never close your eyes when
  I close mine.

I love you
  because you're always
  the same.
You're not in a good mood one day
and a mean mood the next.
  I can always
  count on you being the way
  you are.

I love you
  because you keep on
  loving me,
  even when I say mean things.
Even if I were naughty,
  you would still
  love me.

I love you
  because you make me happy.
I feel a warm fuzzy feeling when
  I'm with you.

And do you know what,
Teddy Bear,
I guess I love God because
   He never argues or fights with me.
   He never says mean things about me.
   He's always there when I need a friend.
   He always seems to have a smile
      for me,
      at least when I'm good.
   He never runs away, he's always there.
   He's lovable and huggable.
   He watches over me all night while
      I'm asleep.
   He's always the same.
   He keeps on loving me, even when I'm
      not lovable.
   He makes me happy
      and gives me
      wonderful warm feelings
      when he's with me.
   He does many, many more
      wonderful things
      that a little Teddy Bear
      can't do.

Thank you,
Teddy Bear,
   for being so
   wonderful.
That's why
I love you.

Thank you,
dear God,
  for being
  much, much
    more wonderful.

That's why I love you
  much, much more
  than even my wonderful
  Teddy Bear.

56

*That
Million-Dollar
Something*

There's a million-dollar something
that I am looking for.
It's worth at least a million,
or maybe even more.

It's something that you cannot find
in any super store.
But that million-dollar something
makes you want a million more.

You can't stuff that million something
in your pocket, purse or shoe.
It's something you can't wash or wear,
it's something you can't chew.

246

That million-dollar something
  makes you feel that you're brand-new.
I especially want this something
  if it comes to me from you.

You must not miss that marvelous thing
  and feel you're really smug.
It's worth too much to rent or buy
  in bag or box or jug.

That million-dollar something
  is as snuggly as a rug,
because, my darling Mommy dear,
  it's your million-dollar hug!

57

The
Tear
Wiper

Dawn and her dad always had a little talk before bed time. Dawn usually told Dad the good things that happened that day, and the not-so-good things, too.

"I fell down when I was roller skating," said Dawn. "It really hurt! I cried a little."

"I'm sorry you hurt," said Dad. "If Mother or I had been there, we would have given you a big hug."

"Some kids made fun of me at school this morning," Dawn said. "I cried even more than when I fell."

"That's a different kind of hurt," said Dad.

"Hurting our hearts can be more painful than hurting our bodies."

"Then, on the way home from school, that big dog down the street came out and barked at me," Dawn added. "I was so scared. I cried then, too."

Dad thought a minute or two. "Mother and I can't be there to hug you every time you get hurt," he said. "We would if we could, but we can't."

"I know that," said Dawn. "But I wish someone could hug me each time I cry."

"You need a Tear Wiper," said Dad.

"What's a Tear Wiper?" asked Dawn.

"Someone to wipe away your tears when you cry." said Dad. "You need someone to comfort you and make you feel better when you hurt."

"Do you mean someone I could carry in my pocket?" asked Dawn. "He would have to be very small. Are there mice-like Tear Wipers?"

"Pretend ones, perhaps," said Dad. "But there is a better one than that."

Dawn looked puzzled. "What is it?" she asked. "Who is it?"

"There's a Tear Wiper who is always with you," said Dad.

"There is?" asked Dawn. "Where? Who?"

"Each time you get hurt, he will make you feel better if you ask him," Dad added.

"I want to ask him," said Dawn. "But who is he?"

"His name is Jesus," said Dad. "You can't carry him in your pocket. You don't need to. But he always goes with you. Next time you get hurt, ask him to comfort you. Ask him to be your Tear Wiper."

"I will, I will," said Dawn.

So Dawn prayed to her Tear Wiper right then. And she asked Jesus to wipe away her tears for that day. She asked Jesus to comfort her. Do you think he did?

58

*Why
Do I
Sleep?*

"Time for bed," said Mom. "Dad and I will come and tuck you in."

"Why do I have to go to bed?" asked Rita. "Why do I have to sleep, anyway?"

"I've wondered that, too," said Dad. "Sometimes we wish we could just keep on playing or reading or talking. Why sleep?"

"Well, why do we sleep?" asked Rita. "Why can't I stay up all night?"

"Want to try?" asked Dad. He had seen Rita yawn three times on the way to her bedroom.

Rita yawned again. "Some other night,"

she said with a smile. Rita knew that she would not stay awake very long.

"But why do I sleep?" Rita asked again.

Dad smiled this time. "I guess you deserve an answer," he said. "You have asked three times. Rita, I don't know all that happens to us while we sleep. We dream, and God must help us do that for a good reason. I think there are a lot of other good things that happen while we sleep. We don't even know some. Now, let's pretend."

"Let's pretend that I start our car and run it full speed all day. Then I never turn it off. I keep it running fast all night and all the next day. It just keeps on running full speed, day after day. What do you think will happen to that car?"

"I think that poor car might wear out fast," said Rita. "Or it might get tired and crash."

"I think so, too," said Dad. "Let's pretend again."

"Let's pretend that you're a cowgirl, riding on a fast horse. Because he's fast, you make him keep running as fast as he can all day and all night and all the next day. That poor horse never stops. He just keeps running at full speed. What do you think will happen to that horse?"

"I think that poor horse might fall over and die," said Rita.

"I think so, too," said Dad. "Horses must rest like cars and kids. But let's pretend once more."

"Let's pretend that there is a dear little girl named Rita. She likes to run and play. Because she likes to do that, she keeps on running and playing all day. Then she keeps on all night and all the next day. She never stops running and playing. What do you think will happen to that dear little girl?"

"I think she will wear out fast," said Rita. "She may even crash like the car."

"I think so, too," said Dad. "Kids must rest like cars and horses. So God gives us sleep to help us turn off our tired bodies and minds. It's like turning off the car lights. The battery lasts longer!"

Rita yawned. "Are you through?" she asked. "I'm tired. I want to go to sleep."

"Good night, Rita," said Dad.

"Good night, Rita," said Mom.

"Good niii . . . . . zzzzz," said Rita.